Are You an Art Sleuth?

Are You an Art Sleuth?

LOOK, DISCOVER, LEARN!

Brooke DiGiovanni Evans

Quarto is the authority on a wide range of topics.
Quarto educates, entertains and enriches the lives of our readers—enthusiasts and lovers of hands-on living.
www.QuartoKnows.com

First published in the United States of America in 2016 by
Rockport Publishers, an Imprint of
Quarto Publishing Group USA Inc.
100 Cummings Center, Suite 406-L
Beverly, Massachusetts 01915-6101
Telephone: (978) 282-9590
Fax: (978) 283-2742
QuartoKnows.com
Visit our blogs at QuartoKnows.com

10 9 8 7 6 5 4 3 2 1

ISBN: 978-1-63159-131-0

Digital edition published in 2016
eISBN: 978-1-63159-195-2

Library of Congress Cataloging-in-Publication Data available.

Design: Allison Meierding
Illustrations: Allison Meierding
Page Layout: Laura H. Couallier, Laura Herrmann Design
Cover Images: Bridgeman Images

Printed in China

DEDICATION

To Darren, for endless encouragement, advice, and editorial notes.

To my parents, for telling me to follow my passion and to study art.

To Barbara, for giving me this opportunity and many others.

To Daniel, Leo, and Naomi, who I hope will enjoy this book someday.

CONTENTS

Henri Rousseau
1892

INTRODUCTION

Are You an Art Sleuth?

You probably are. In fact I'm sure you are. Go ahead, try it. Take a look at one of the paintings in this book. Then go back and look again—really closely this time. You'll see things you didn't notice the first time. You'll discover that even though a painting is made on the surface of a canvas or a piece of wood, the picture seems to go deep beyond the surface. You'll discover in your sleuthing that the things you notice aren't just in the foreground where the people and objects are the largest, but way in the back of the painting, too. Look at the hills and trees in the distance; look through windows to the outdoors, through doorways into the next room, look at what's reflected in mirrors, and what people are doing in the back of a crowd. The artist put things there on purpose and wanted you to find them.

You'll find something else, too, when you look at a painting very closely. You'll discover what the world was like in different places and at different times. You'll meet children who play with hoops and children who wear lace caps. You'll meet a whole town of people who turn out to go skating when the river freezes, and ladies who go fishing in their best silk gowns. They all have something to tell you about their lives.

The paintings in this book come from twenty-one museums around the world. With each painting there's a list of things to search for and find. Then turn the page and learn more about the picture and its story. Art is full of stories and secrets. Every painting has a lot to share with the art sleuths who take the time to look very closely.

It's Raining

Don't let a rainy day spoil your sleuthing. Try to find:

11 hands

8 hats

2 gloves

1 pocket handkerchief

9 umbrellas

2 white shirt cuffs

1 bracelet

3 beards

Les Parapluies (The Umbrellas),
Pierre-Auguste Renoir (French, 1841–1919)
Dublin City Gallery, The Hugh Lane, Ireland
Bridgeman Images

Auguste Renoir, *Les Parapluies*

A *Parapluie?*

Wait, what's a *parapluie*? Can you guess from looking at the painting? It's the word for "umbrella" in French. Here are some other ways to say it. In Italian an umbrella is a *parapioggia*, in German it's a *regenschirm*, and in Spanish it's a *paraguas.*

It's time to go outside —oh no, it's raining!

Grab your rain gear: coat, hat, boots, and *parapluie*!

What can this rainy day painting tell you? Let's find out.

Paris in the 1800s

So many people on this very busy street. Are they dressed for hot weather or cold? What makes you think so? One woman is carrying a box. What do you suppose is in it? Are all these people going somewhere special?

Will the Sun Come Out?

Do you think the rain has stopped or just started? The woman at the front of the painting is lifting her dress to protect it from puddles—but she forgot her *parapluie*! Look at the woman's face in the middle of the painting. She's checking the sky. Do you think she is taking down her umbrella or putting it up? Do you see any raindrops?

A Gray Day

Did you know you can show what kind of weather it is by choosing certain colors? Auguste Renoir used a lot of gray, black, and blue in the painting to make it feel like a rainy day. If this were a sunny day, what colors do you think he would have used instead?

A Moment in Time

Renoir was an Impressionist artist. The Impressionists liked to paint everyday moments from life, especially outdoors in natural light: a busy street, a sunny day, a group of people dancing. This looks like one of those moments. If you were to draw a busy moment from your life to show Monsieur Renoir, what would you draw?

Start and Stop

It took Renoir six years to finish this painting! He started it, then stopped, and came back to it later. The little girl in the front might have been four years old when he started the painting. How old would she have been when he finished? Have you ever started a picture and then stopped? Did you go back to it later and finish it up?

Rolling Hoops

The little girl wearing high-button shoes in this picture has a rolling hoop toy. To play with it you need to balance the hoop and keep it rolling, using a stick to push it along. When it starts going fast, you have to run to keep up with it. Children in the 1880s loved this game. If you have a hula hoop and a stick at home, you can try it yourself. And if it's raining don't forget to bring your *parapluie*!

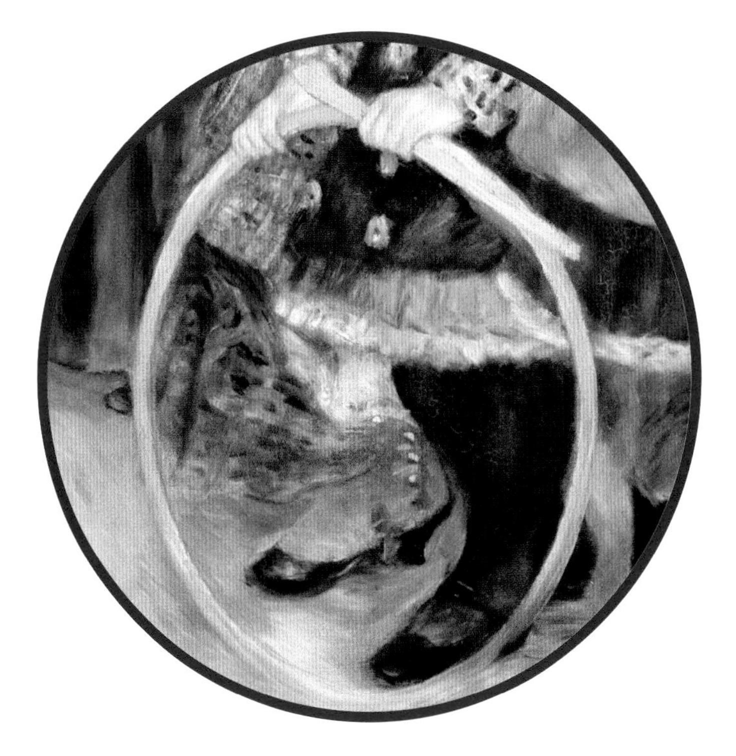

Let's Go to the Park

Your sleuthing eyes will have to look deep into the distance for some of these things:

3 dogs

1 trumpet

2 fishing poles

1 folding fan

1 monkey

1 bouquet

9 open parasols

1 butterfly

A Sunday Afternoon on the Island of La Grande Jatte,
Georges Seurat (French, 1859–1891)
Art Institute of Chicago, Chicago, Illinois, U.S.A.
Bridgeman Images

Georges Seurat, *A Sunday Afternoon on the Island of La Grande Jatte*

Family Time

It's a sunny Sunday afternoon! What do you and your family like to do together on a sunny afternoon? In the 1880s, Georges Seurat painted people enjoying a lovely day on the island of La Grande Jatte, which is a park in the middle of the River Seine in Paris, France.

Sunshine. Blue sky. What could be nicer?

A sunny day is a good time to look for small details. Take a look!

Tiny Dots!

Seurat painted this scene in a new way. Look closely and you'll see that the picture is made up of thousands of tiny dots. Step away from the painting and the dots blend together. Seurat was one of the inventors of this type of painting, called Pointillism. (Each dot is a point!) He combined dots in different colors to make the trees, grass, and even the people. How many different colors can you find in the water surrounding the island? He used bright-colored dots to show where the sun was on the grass and dark-colored dots to show the shadows. Where do you think shadows come from? Are they always the same color?

Where Are the Play Clothes?

In the 1880s grown-ups wore hats when they left the house and women always wore long dresses or skirts. Many people dressed in their best clothes and nicest hats on a Sunday afternoon when they'd be seeing friends. Do their clothes look comfortable for a hot summer day? One man took his jacket off. Can you spot him? Do you think you would have fun in the park wearing those kinds of clothes? What would you wear instead? Draw a picture of yourself wearing the perfect hat for the park or carrying a parasol for shade.

How Big Is It?

This painting is over six feet tall and ten feet (1.8 × 3 m) wide—as big as a wall. That's a lot of dots! It took Georges Seurat two years to make this painting. It's so big that you could imagine walking right into the scene. If you could, where would you stand and how would you pose? Imagine running through the park all the way into the distance.

Be a Pointillist

Pretend you're Georges Seurat and create your own Pointillist picture. It's easiest to start with something simple—a cloud in the sky, maybe. Grab a crayon or a marker and start making colored dots on a piece of paper. For the sky you might want to use some light blue dots, then maybe purple, or gray, and white. Look closely at how Seurat created his sky. What colors did he use?

Keeping Count

Art sleuths have to look carefully at the smallest details. Can you find:

3 windows

4 hats

6 rings

1 candle

2 rolls of paper

1 red button

1 glass bottle

1 brick wall

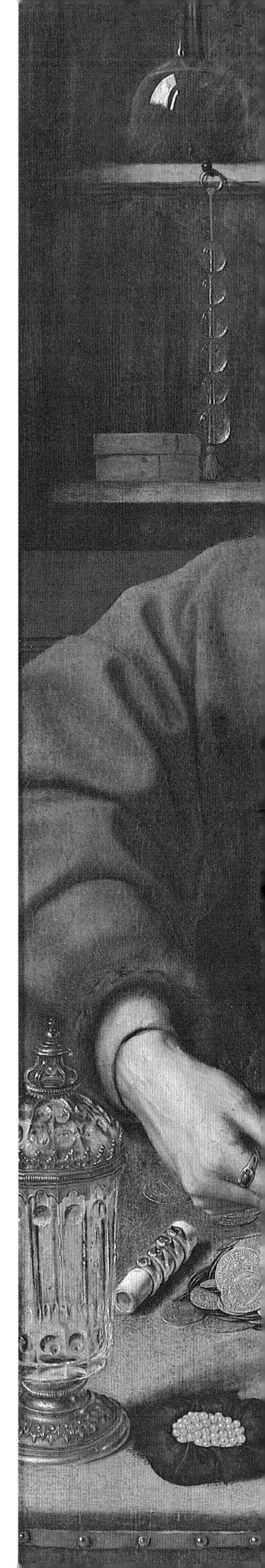

The Moneylender and His Wife,
Quentin Metsys (Belgian, 1466–1530)
Louvre Museum, Paris, France
Bridgeman Images

Quentin Metsys, *The Moneylender and His Wife*

Something interesting is happening here.

This painting shows the indoors, but the artist also shows the outdoors. Can you see how?

What's the Difference?

Life was a lot different five hundred years ago when Quentin Metsys painted this picture. Most shopkeepers were craftsmen or food vendors. And even in the biggest towns there were no banks! If you needed cash, you went to a moneylender like this man, who is working in his shop with his wife looking on. Metsys made the two of them appear very important in this picture by making them so large their elbows don't fit in the painting!

Time for Trade

When people shopped five hundred years ago, they didn't always use money. Sometimes they traded things, saying, "I will give you this, if you will give me that." That's what would happen when you went to see the moneylender. You would offer to trade something in exchange for money. This man is holding a balance scale in his hand. If you gave him a gold ring, he would put it on the scale to find out how much it weighed. Then he would know how much the gold ring was worth. People in Europe didn't have paper money at that time. The man would pay you for your ring with gold and silver coins.

Reflections

Another thing that was different in Quentin Metsys's day was that most people did not have mirrors in their houses. Mirrored glass was a new invention then, and few people had actually seen it. If you had a mirror it would probably be small, very expensive, and you would treasure it as something valuable. Artists were fascinated by mirrors and liked to put them in paintings because they added a touch of magic. They allowed you to see something that wasn't in front of your eyes. There's a man in the mirror in this painting. Could he be the artist? Where do you think he might be sitting? The artist must have used a very fine brush to paint everything in the mirror so small.

What to Wear?

Paintings often tell a lot about the fashions of the day. These people are wearing their hats indoors. Do you think it might be cold outside? Their clothing looks like it might be made out of wool and trimmed with fur at the neck and wrists. The man's coat makes him blend in with the wall behind him. The woman's red gown stands out. You can use color in pictures to make things jump out or fade into the background.

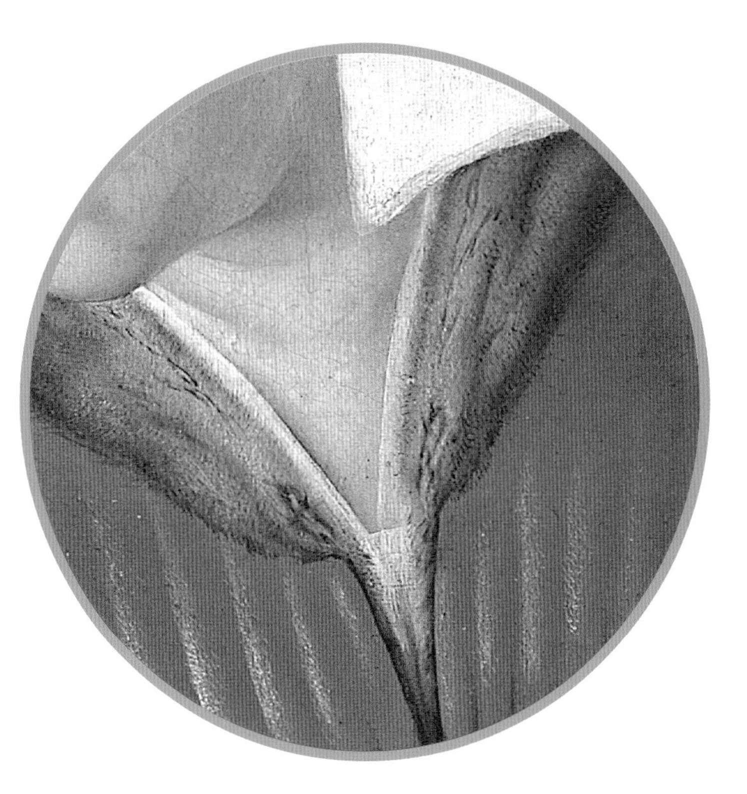

What a Crowd!

Where to look first in this busy scene? Open your sleuthing eyes and find:

1 dog

2 fans

4 parasols

1 spoon

1 cane

2 pairs of eyeglasses

5 black shoes

1 ball

Music in the Tuileries Gardens,
Édouard Manet (French, 1832–1883)
National Gallery, London, UK
Bridgeman Images

Édouard Manet, *Music in the Tuileries Gardens*

Everyone has dressed up in their best for an afternoon of music at the park with their friends and neighbors.

There are still a few seats available, art sleuth! Pull up a chair and get ready for the music.

What's Your Talent?

Édouard Manet was born in Paris, France, in 1832. His father was a lawyer and wanted Édouard to be one, too. But his uncle recognized the boy's interest in art and encouraged his talent by taking him to art classes at the Louvre Museum. Manet became one of the the best known painters of city life in his day.

Painting the Painter

This was one of Manet's first important paintings. It looks old-fashioned now, but in his day, the painting was considered very modern! Manet included portraits of many of his friends and relatives in the crowd and even included a self-portrait. There are lots of men with brown beards and moustaches in the painting. Manet is the bearded man at the far left. Have you ever included all of your friends and family in a drawing? Did you include a portrait of yourself?

Where's the Band?

The Tuileries Gardens are part of a large park in Paris, right next to the Louvre Museum. Today, just as in Manet's day, people gather there on sunny weekends to sit under the chestnut trees and enjoy time with their friends. These people have gathered to listen to some music, but where are the musicians? Everyone is looking out of the painting. They're looking at us! Are you one of the musicians? What instrument would you play?

A Fine Day to Play

The children in this painting may be dressed up in their best white summer outfits for a special day's outing, but they still came prepared to play. Can you find a hoop toy, two pails, and a red, white, and blue ball?

Quiet Time

There are lots of little things hiding in this room. Can you find:

1 dog

1 clock

1 stool

1 bonnet

1 doll hat

1 tiny house

7 dolls

the number 2

The Nursery,
Fritz von Uhde (German, 1848–1911)
Kunsthall, Hamburg, Germany
Bridgeman Images

Fritz von Uhde, *The Nursery*

Come in and play in our room!

Put on your thinking cap, art sleuth. Which girl do you think sleeps in this room? Do the sides on the bed give you a clue?

A Moment in Time

Some artists like to paint famous events or celebrations, but Fritz von Uhde liked to paint pictures of daily life in Germany. He used soft colors to paint a quiet moment during the day for these girls. Their mother is knitting. The oldest girl is sewing, and the others are having fun with their dolls. Even though it's just an ordinary day, von Uhde made it special by putting in so many small details. He painted the girls' toys and doll clothes, their drawings, and paper garlands, as though every one of them was important. That's something to think about when you are drawing: little details can make something seem important.

Inside Out

One of the ways that artists can tell you extra things about the people they paint is by including open windows and doors in a picture. We know a lot about these girls and their home life by looking at their things in this bedroom. But we also know a little bit about what kind of neighborhood they lived in and what their street was like by looking out the window. If you drew a picture of yourself in your bedroom, what would we see outside your window?

Telling Details

Von Uhde painted some details in this scene that are fun for an art sleuth to look for. For instance, we don't know exactly what time of year this is, but we do know the weather was warm. How do we know? If you guessed the open window, you'd be right. There's a lot of sunshine coming in through the window, but is it morning or afternoon? Did you guess "afternoon"? Right again. How do we know? Find the clock on the wall. The time is ten past four. Is this room on the ground floor of the house or on the second floor? It's the second floor. How do we know? Look out the window at the house across the street. The neighbor's window is above the front door.

A Long Time Ago

This scene was painted in 1889. That's a long time ago. In 1889 there were few cars and no planes—these girls would have traveled on trains or by horse and carriage. Women wore long dresses: you can see the mother's striped skirt if you look under the table. Girls wore pinafores, a type of apron, over their dresses to keep their clothes clean. You couldn't just toss your clothes in the washing machine in 1889—they had to be washed by hand. It was important to keep your clothes clean as long as possible. Two of the girls in this painting are wearing pinafores.

Time to say good-bye to these girls, but before you do, put on your sleuthing cap and find the artist's signature.

What's Everyone Doing?

There's a lot going on in this rocky landscape and a lot to look for. See if you can find:

1 fox

4 caves

3 faces in windows

5 books

1 fish

3 riders

2 baskets

1 tiny castle

Thebaide (detail),
The Florentine Master, attributed to Fra Angelico (Tuscan, 1395–1455)
Uffizi Gallery, Florence, Italy
Bridgeman Images

Fra Angelico, *Thebaide* (detail)

Such a busy landscape! What's happening in this painting with all of these tiny people on the other side of the river?

Take a look. See if you can spot the quickest way across the river.

So Many Things to Do

Fra Angelico painted in Italy during the 1400s. (*Fra* means "brother.") In this painting he included many small scenes to discover. Can you find the man washing someone's feet? How about the man sitting at a table with a jug, a knife, and a loaf of bread? Do you think he'll give his dog a treat? Why do you suppose one man is ringing a bell? Is it time for lunch? Can you find a man in a tree?

Animals and Caves

There are a lot of other things besides people in this painting. How many different kinds of animals can you find? Do you see any birds? What about a man riding on the back of an animal with spots? The rocky landscape also has a number of caves and it looks like people live inside them! Would you like to live in a cave? Draw a picture of what your room in the cave would look like.

Tiny Buildings

One thing that's fun about drawing and painting is that you can make things any size you like. Fra Angelico knew that. Do you notice anything strange about the size of the houses he painted in this picture? They're the same size as the people! Some of the houses are too small to even sit inside. The boats are very small, too. At the bottom left of the painting, a man takes up nearly the entire space inside his boat, and another man is climbing in to join him! What will happen next? Will they both fit or will the boat tip over?

Step Inside

Fra Angelico used his imagination to create this painting. The setting is the Egyptian city of Thebes, but Fra Angelico lived in Italy and never visited this city. Grab some paper and pencils and create your own imaginative landscape with many different small scenes. Will you draw a place you've never seen, or a place that you know? Will there be caves and people in trees? If you follow Fra Angelico's example and make the houses and cars really small, you could draw your entire neighborhood in one picture. Who will be in each scene? What will they be doing?

Lunchtime Is Over

Time to play! Can things hide in the bright sunshine? Let's find out. Be an art sleuth and search for:

1 hat with white roses

1 hat with red trim

2 drinking glasses

1 open parasol

1 closed parasol

2 fruit bowls

1 wooden toy

the loaf's missing piece of bread

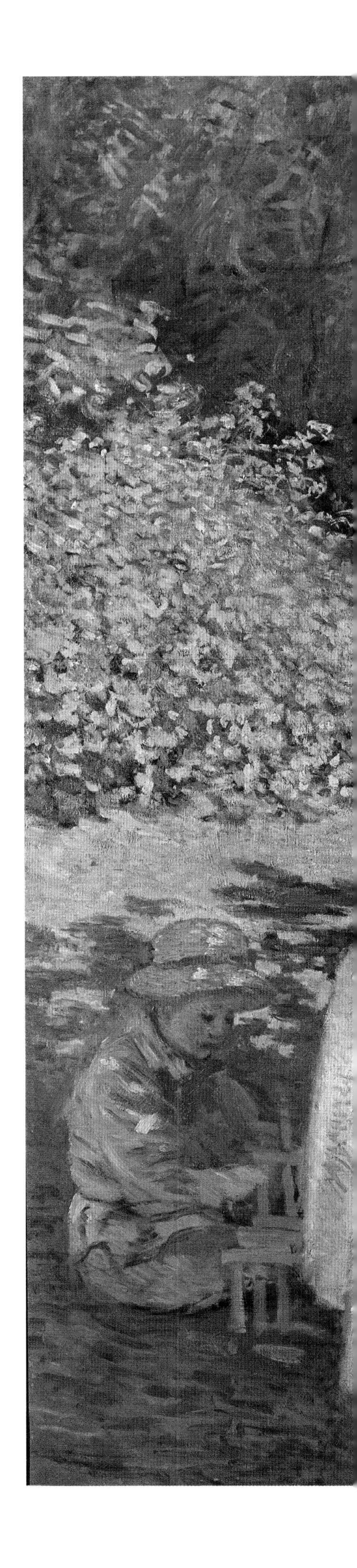

The Luncheon,
Claude Monet (French, 1840–1926)
Musée d'Orsay, Paris, France
Bridgeman Images

Claude Monet, *The Luncheon*

It's a beautiful, sunny day for playing outside.

Would you like to discover more about the little boy playing in the painting? He grew up to be a chemist, a kind of scientist.

Painting Outside

Imagine stepping into this painting with flowers all around and sunshine on your face. Claude Monet loved to capture the feeling of sunny days in his paintings. He was part of a group of artists called the Impressionists. Before Monet's time, artists usually painted inside their studios, but the Impressionists liked to go outside to paint. Monet painted his garden over and over again, at different times of day and at different times of the year. He liked to see how the garden changed when the sunlight changed. Can you tell where the sunlight is falling in this painting? Monet used light colors to make the sunlight feel warm and dark colors to make the shade feel cool.

Let's Go for a Stroll

The little boy's mother, Camille, is in the background of the painting. She's taking a stroll with a friend and enjoying the flowers. Claude Monet used colorful dabs of paint to create the flowers. He didn't try to paint every petal, but focused on the colors you'd see in a blooming garden. If you look closely you'll see that he combined many colors for each flower—red, orange, white. The colors in this painting make it feel like summer. What colors would you see in the fall or winter?

Favorite Toys

It's easier to see things in the sunlight than it is in the shade, but Jean, the artist's son, doesn't seem to mind. He's sitting in the shade, building with his wooden blocks. In Jean's time there was no electricity and nothing digital. Children played with toys like blocks, marbles, tops, hoops, dolls, and jump ropes. Jean seems too busy with his blocks to notice what anyone else is doing. But his father had to be nearby with his easel and paints! Where do you think Claude Monet was standing when he painted this picture?

What's Left to Eat?

All that's left on the table are the remains of the fruit dessert, but this was a fancy lunch! The table is set with a white cloth, pretty china dishes, and a silver teapot. If you ate outside, would you have a picnic, a cookout, or a fancy lunch like this one? Think about what you would like to eat and serve your guests at your outdoor lunch. Draw a picture of your feast.

Picnic Time

It's too nice to stay indoors. Let's play outside and try to find:

1 blue bow

1 berry necklace

1 peach in hand

1 ring

1 basket

1 headband

2 spoons

a hat that's turned into a bowl

The Children's Holiday,
(Portrait of Mrs. Thomas Fairbairn and Her Children)
William Holman Hunt (English, 1827–1910)
Torre Abbey, Torquay, Devon, England
Bridgeman Images

William Holman Hunt, *The Children's Holiday*

A Lot to Carry

Mrs. Fairbairn, the mother in this picture, must have had a lot of help carrying this picnic to the park. It's easy to spot the red leather chair, fancy silver, and fine tea things, but can your sleuthing eyes find an Oriental rug?

What's nice about having lunch outdoors?

Look at all the things the Fairbairn children have found to do!

Let in the Light

All artists pay close attention to light in their paintings. Hunt was very careful to put light-colored things next to dark-colored ones in every part of this painting. Even the shadows under the trees are like light and dark stripes. This helps all of the details stand out.

Don't Paint My Picture!

The two young deer in this painting seem almost tame and very curious about the picnic. They're not afraid to pose for the family portrait. Can you find another animal that is much shyer?

I Painted It—Honest!

William Holman Hunt and his fellow artists believed that making paintings as realistic as possible made them more honest. Look at the different parts of this painting and discover all of the details that Hunt painted realistically: The feather on the hat looks like it would really feel like a feather if you ran your fingers over it; the bark on the trees looks like it would be very rough on your hands; and it looks like he painted every single leaf on the trees. What other textures can you find in Hunt's painting?

Strap on Your Skates

Here's a busy winter scene. Which way to look first? Strap on your skates and try to find:

3 horses

1 missing hat

1 ladder

1 boat with a sail

1 oar

1 axe

1 sign with a crescent moon

1 horse with a plume

Winter Landscape with Ice Skaters (detail),
Hendrick Avercamp (Dutch, 1585–1634)
Rijksmuseum, Amsterdam, Netherlands
Bridgeman Images

Hendrick Avercamp, *Winter Landsape with Ice Skaters* (detail)

Grab a warm hat, scarf, and gloves. It's cold enough to go skating!

Hmm. That's interesting. When you look at it, a frozen river is almost like a road!

Time for Skating

As far as your eye can see in this painting there are people enjoying the winter weather. They are skating and sledding on a frozen river. Skating was a very popular winter activity in the Netherlands, where Hendrick Avercamp lived. In the 1600s the winters were extremely cold and the ice was thick enough for horses and sleighs to travel on. What would you use to travel across the ice on a frozen river?

See Your Reflection

Have you ever looked at your reflection in a lake or a pond? It can be almost like looking in a mirror. Ice does the same thing. Look at the horse and red sled in this painting, then at the ice below them. Can you spot the reflections? Can you find any others?

Puffy Skirts and Petticoats

The winter clothing in this painting looks a little different from what you wear. In the 1600s men wore a jacket and britches that ended at their knees and then stockings to cover their lower legs. Women wore puffy skirts and petticoats. Some people are on the ice in their finest clothing. Everyone is wearing a hat. Can you spot a hat with two orange feathers?

Off in the Distance

This picture is painted on a flat piece of wood, but it looks like you can see way down the river. How did the artist do that? Here's an art sleuth clue: artists create distance by making the people in the front of the painting big, then gradually smaller, until they're so tiny you can barely see them.

Winter Fun!

Hendrick Avercamp liked to skate with his parents when he was a child. What do you like to do in the winter? Skating? Sledding? Drinking hot chocolate? Draw your favorite winter activity. Will it be inside or outside? Will you include lots of people like Avercamp did?

Stop, Thief!

Everyone's eyes are busy in this painting! Open your sleuthing eyes to find:

1 coin

2 rabbits

1 earring

1 clipper

1 gold bracelet

2 birds

1 knife in a sheath

1 gold clasp

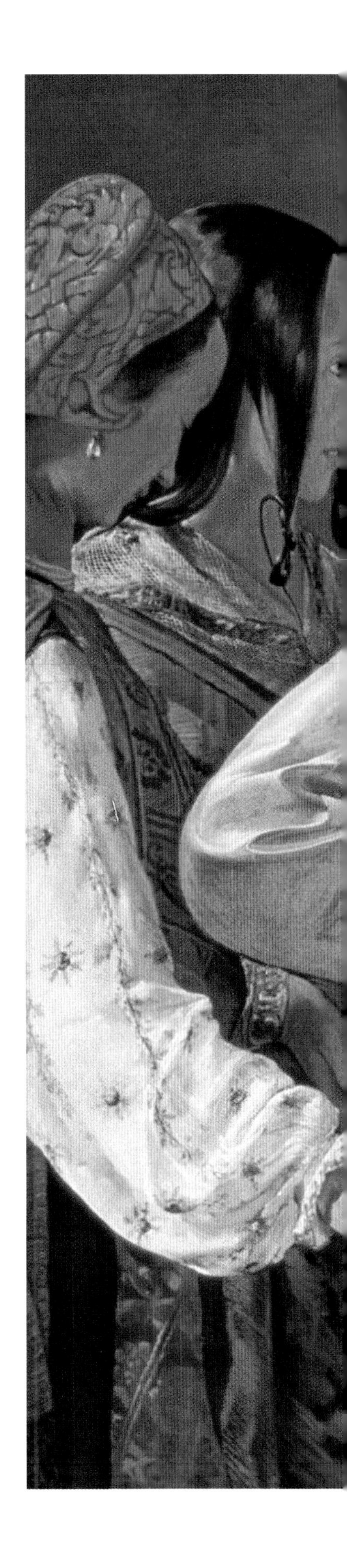

The Fortune Teller,
Georges de La Tour (French, 1593–1652)
Metropolitan Museum of Art, New York, U.S.A.
Bridgeman Images

Georges de la Tour, *The Fortune Teller*

What's happening in this painting? Use your art-sleuthing skills to discover a crime!

Look at the ladies' faces, art sleuth. Do you think they're having fun?

So Sneaky!

Oh, no! While the young man is about to have his fortune told by the old woman, the other women are up to no good. One is reaching into his pocket and another is cutting his golden chain! They're stealing from him! What would you say to warn him?

Eyes Are the Clue

Look closely at the eyes in this painting. The man is looking at the old woman who is looking back at him. She's holding the silver coin he's paid her to tell his fortune. She's talking to him so that he pays attention only to her. The woman cutting the chain is facing us, but she's not looking at us. Her sneaky eyes are watching the man's face to make sure he doesn't notice her hands. The woman stealing from his pocket is looking down, as if she's not paying any attention to him at all. Georges de La Tour told a story with eyes. You can, too. Try drawing sneaky eyes, happy eyes, and sad eyes.

Beautiful Clothes

In the 1600s when Georges de La Tour was painting, people liked to wear rich-looking clothing. Men's clothes were as pretty as women's. The young man in this painting has a belt with a bow, silky sleeves, and a fancy, embroidered collar. Such pretty things were expensive and wearing them showed how wealthy you were.

Fancy Fabric

Great sailing ships traveled between Europe and the East, bringing back beautiful fabric that was made into clothing. You can see some of it in this picture. The cloth in the old woman's dress is woven with animals, birds, and vases. The other women are wearing clothing trimmed with gold. They are very fancy thieves. Do you think they'll get away with their crime?

Dark Shadows

De La Tour made this picture very dark with gloomy shadows. The two women on the left almost fade into the darkness. If these five people were standing outdoors in the bright sunshine, would the picture still look as sneaky and dangerous? If they were outdoors, someone else might see what was happening and stop the women. The darkness helps hide what the women are doing.

Pesky Monsters

There are some very funny things happening in this painting. Look closely for:

2 ladders

1 tiny bow and arrow

1 spilling jug

1 armed funnel

3 bridges

2 bells

the letter T

Anthony's eyeglasses

The Temptation of Saint Anthony,
Hieronymus Bosch (Dutch, 1450–1516)
Prado Museum, Madrid, Spain
Bridgeman Images

Hieronymus Bosch, *The Temptation of Saint Anthony*

Anthony is doing some serious thinking in this landscape filled with pesky monsters!

Look at those monsters. Do you suppose they're making noise? What do you think they sound like?

Creatures!

Hieronymus Bosch painted during the 1400s—600 years ago. Everyone who sees Bosch's paintings remembers the funny-looking monsters he created. There are some pretty strange ones in this scene. Search for the monster that looks like a building with arms. What do you think that monster looks like when it walks? How about the one in the lower corner with a turtle-like head? Those monsters are trying to interrupt Anthony's thoughts!

Where to Sleep?

Anthony has made a shelter for himself on the hillside, using the old tree and a straw roof to protect him from the rain. Do you think that would be a comfortable place to sleep? Or would you rather sleep in one of the houses down the hill?

Your Very Own Monsters

Grab some paper and pencils and create your own monsters. Will they be big or small? Friendly, scary, or just plain silly? Will they have heads and legs from different creatures like Bosch's monsters? Will they disturb you when you're trying to think?

A Piggy Pet

Stories about Anthony say that he took care of pigs when he was a young man. In paintings, he is often shown with a pig as his pet and traveling companion. This one has a pretty little bell in her ear and doesn't seem to be paying any attention to the monster next to her. Do you think a pig would make a good pet? What animal would you choose as your traveling companion?

Above and Below

In this picture Anthony is sitting on a hill. How can you tell? Everything on top of the hill with Anthony is big, and everything below him is tiny. There are more hills in the distance, too. The next time you stand on a hill, or a mountain, or high up in a sky-scraper, look down and you'll see that everything below you looks small. You can draw things that way in your own pictures, too.

Trees in the Desert?

Bosch thought he was painting the desert when he made this picture, but he had never seen a desert. He lived in the Netherlands, where there is lots of water and farm-land, so his desert has trees, grass, streams, and little flowering plants. What's fun about drawing and painting is that you can make things look any way you like. Try drawing a place that you've never seen—like the moon. What does it look like in your imagination?

Beep! Honk! Beep!

It looks like traffic has stopped for the moment. There's just enough time for you to discover:

5 wheels

1 green hat

1 steering wheel

1 white hat band

3 lamps

1 white collar

the number 19 twice

the word "room"

Piccadilly Circus,
Charles Ginner (British, 1878–1952)
Courtesy of Tate Britain, London, England

CLAPHAM JUNCTION [19] HIGHBURY
THE
NEW
REVUE
ROOM
5834
BLOOMSBURY ANGEL
HYDE PARK

Charles Ginner, *Piccadilly Circus*

Where's the Circus?

Charles Ginner painted Piccadilly Circus on a busy afternoon, but this doesn't look like other circuses you've seen, does it? Where are the acrobats and clowns? "Circus" is another word for "circle," and this circus is a traffic circle. Piccadilly Circus is a famous (and very busy) part of the city of London.

Imagine stepping into this painting. Cars and buses are all around you. What would it sound like?

Did you notice something interesting about the tires on the cars and buses, art sleuth? They're just like bicycle tires!

And What's a Piccadilly?

A "piccadill" is the name for a type of collar that well-dressed men and women wore in the 1600s. A famous tailor who made these collars had his shop near the street where Piccadilly Circus is now. That's where the name came from. If you named your street after something you like to wear, what would it be called? Blue Jeans Lane? Tee-Shirt Circle?

Oops! Bump! Tight Squeeze!

How do you make things look really busy in a picture? Ginner knew. You make it so crowded that nothing quite fits on the page! We can only see half of the car and part of the big red bus. The flower seller is squeezed into the middle, the woman in black looks like she's just about to step out of view, and the people on the upper deck of the bus look like they could hit their heads on the top of the painting! Ouch! Try arranging your toys far apart, then arrange them all bunched up together and see which arrangement looks busier.

Would You Like to Buy a Flower?

In the middle of all the traffic, a woman is making bouquets to sell to people passing by. She's wearing her hat and apron, ready for business. The women who sold flowers and things to eat all over London were called coster girls. What else could you buy from them? Here's a hint: costers (or costards) are a kind of apple!

Living in London

Charles Ginner liked to paint everyday scenes in London. His paintings show us what life was like in the early 1900s. When he did this painting, more than 100 years ago, things were a lot different than now. In 1912 people started their cars with a crank instead of a key. If you look at the front of the green car, under the engine, you'll see the crank. What else in the picture is different from today?

What's your favorite place to visit? How do you get there? Car, taxi, train, or bicycle maybe? How about the top of a double-decker bus?

It's a Party!

With so many people, things could get lost! It will take a careful sleuth to find:

1 pen and paper

1 bird

8 red hats

1 pair of knee socks

1 set of folded arms in front

1 set of folded arms in back

1 baby

2 purses on strings

The Peasants' Wedding,
Pieter Brueghel the Younger (Flemish, c. 1564–1636)
Art Gallery of Ontario, Toronto, Canada
Bridgeman Images

Pieter Brueghel the Younger, *The Peasants' Wedding*

Let's celebrate! Someone's getting married!

The dancers look lively. But look at the musicians' faces. Do you think they're getting tired?

Music and Merriment

Imagine you've landed in the middle of this wedding celebration. What would it sound like? Two men are playing a dancing tune on their bagpipes and everyone is having fun. With so many people it must be noisy.

A Painting Family

Pieter Brueghel the Younger came from a family of painters. His father (the Elder) was a painter and so were his brother and son. We know a lot about what the lives of ordinary people looked like in northern Europe 400 years ago because of Brueghel's paintings. He liked painting pictures of peasant life. Peasants worked hard, farming the land and taking care of their animals. But when it was time to take a break and celebrate exciting events like a wedding, they knew how to have a good time.

A Peasant Wedding

This doesn't look like weddings today. For one thing, the bride, seated at the table, is wearing a black dress. It would be her very best dress with its lace collar and cuffs. Peasants did not have a lot of money, so they wore whatever clothes they had to a wedding. The bride's guests are putting coins on the plate in front of her as wedding gifts, and a man is writing it all down.

A Painting Trick

Brueghel was an expert at squeezing a lot of people into a painting. Try drawing this many people in one picture sometime—it's tricky. Here's how he did it. He painted this scene as if he were sitting on a branch of a tree, looking down at the crowd. That way, he only had to show the heads and shoulders of the people clustered in the back of the painting, not their arms and legs. He also used lots of colors for their clothing, and many kinds of hats, so that everyone stands out.

Ready to Dance?

There doesn't seem to be one special dance that everyone is doing. Some people are holding hands, some are turning, and others are dancing back to back. Try dancing with your hands on your hips like the man and woman in the front.

Where Are You?

If you've ever played hide-and-seek, you already know what it's like to be a sleuth! Seek and find:

4 children

1 open door

2 headbands

3 mirrors

2 teacups

1 black shoe

3 masks

a wrinkle in the rug

Hide and Seek,
Jacques (James) Tissot (French, 1836–1902)
National Gallery, Washington, D.C., U.S.A.
Bridgeman Images

Jacques (James) Tissot, *Hide and Seek*

An Artist's Studio

These people have gathered in James Tissot's painting studio in London, England. You can't see him, but when he was painting this picture he would have been standing just about where you are sitting, enjoying the scene.

Ready, set, pose!

Here's something interesting, art sleuth. This painting is almost like a photograph, but when the artist painted it, photographs were not in color!

Soft, Hard, Fuzzy

Tissot filled his studio with all kinds of things that he might use in a painting—comfortable furniture, pretty rugs, vases, pillows, and blankets. He has painted everything very carefully so that your eyes tell you what it feels like. Which things look soft? Which things look hard?

You're "It"

Do you think the little girl in the white dress with orange ribbons will find the others? She looks like she's going after the ball on the floor instead. If you could give her some hints where to look and what to do, what would you tell her? Can you spot any other places in the room that would be good places to hide?

Lighting a Painting

Light is important to artists. They can't paint without it—it's just as important as paint and brushes. Tissot has a lot of tall windows and glass doors in his studio to let in plenty of sunlight. Can you find any places inside the studio where the sunlight has fallen? Here's a hint: look at the mirrors, the shiny surfaces of furniture, and the children's faces. Look around the room you're sitting in. What looks shinier, the hard surfaces or the soft surfaces?

Step Inside

It's fun to have everyone together. Which room do you and your family like to spend time in together? Is it a good room for hide-and-seek? If you drew a picture of your family doing something together, would you be having dinner? Playing a game? Reading stories? A picture is a good way of telling stories.

Ahoy There!

This busy seaport has lots going on. It's the perfect spot for an art sleuth to do some snooping. Try to find:

1 red dog collar

1 bird

1 man on a mast

1 round roof

2 pieces of paper

2 feathered helmets

1 man on a bridge

some people in windows

The Arrival of Saint Ursula,
Vittore Carpaccio (Italian, c. 1465–1525/26)
Accademia Gallery, Venice, Italy
Bridgeman Images

Vittore Carpaccio, *The Arrival of Saint Ursula*

Land ho! It's a cloudy, gray day in Cologne, Germany, and a large ship has just arrived. Let's see what's going on.

How many ships can you spy, art sleuth?

Let's Go to Sea

Traveling by ship was an important way to get to places in the 1400s, when Vittore Carpaccio painted this picture. Roads were terrible in those days. Most roads were simply dirt that turned into mud when it rained. People preferred to travel by ship, and they sent food and other supplies that way, too. All of the most important cities were built on rivers or had ocean ports.

Ships Ahoy!

Can you see other ships sailing in? They look smaller because they are still far away. Ships did not have engines in the 1400s. Sailors relied on the wind filling the sails to make their ship move. The stronger the wind, the faster the ship could go. And if there was no wind? Nothing moved! How can you tell that the wind is blowing in this picture? Look at the flags and pennants on the buildings and masts. They're all going in the same direction. That's because of the wind.

Ship to Shore

A young man has rowed a small boat to the ship to help Ursula to shore. With all the soldiers and guards nearby, she'll have plenty of people to escort her safely to the castle. Ursula was the daughter of a king and she was supposed to marry a very powerful leader—but she refused. This got her in a lot of trouble!

Anybody Home?

Did you spot the people in the castle windows? What do you think Ursula will see when she gets inside? Many castles were like small towns inside their walls. Lots of people lived there, not just kings and queens. There were cooks, ladies-in-waiting, blacksmiths, knights, servants, stable boys, and more. If you lived inside a castle's walls, what would you want to be? Draw a picture of yourself in your castle, looking out of a window.

Tell a Story

Ursula lived a long time before Vittore Carpaccio painted this picture —nearly 1,000 years before! That's something to remember when you want to tell a story with drawings or paintings: you don't have to make a picture about someone you know. You can make a picture and tell a story about someone from a long time ago.

Hold That Pose

These children look like they're ready to have some fun. Join them and see if you can find:

2 gray ears

1 tiny angel

2 birds

1 wheel

1 cookie

2 buckles

2 bunches of cherries

1 pointed toe

The Graham Children,
William Hogarth (British, 1697–1764)
National Gallery, London, England
Bridgeman Images

William Hogarth, *The Graham Children*

Say cheese—it's time for a family picture!
These children are on their best behavior for their portait. You can discover something about manners in the 1700s in this painting. Anna Maria is making a curtsy for the painter. A boy, in her place, would have made a bow.

Family Portrait

The Graham children—Henrietta Catherine, Anna Maria, Richard Robert, and baby Thomas—are posing for their portrait. Their father worked for King George II as an apothecary (someone who makes medicine). During the 1700s only important people could afford to have their portrait painted. Working for the king was an important job.

Sit Still, Please

Next time you pose for a photo, imagine having to sit for many hours while the picture is taken. That's what the Graham children had to do. There were no cameras in their day. They had to hold still so that William Hogarth could make many drawings of them. Then he used the sketches to create this painting. Try holding the pose of Anna Maria (in the middle of the painting) for a long time.

Dress-Up Time

The Graham children wore their fanciest clothes for this portrait. The two girls are wearing silk dresses. Richard Robert, the older boy, wears britches and a jacket just like the clothes grown men would wear. His younger brother, Thomas, is in a dress. In those days, boys wore dresses until they were at least two years old.

Meow!

What is that cat doing? She looks like she's ready to pounce. Richard Robert is playing a bird-organ: when he turned the handle, it played bird songs. The bird in the cage might be singing in response to the music. The cat has taken notice. What do you think will happen next? There's another bird in this painting. Did you spot it?

Draw a picture of your family. Think about how everyone will pose. Will you be serious or silly? What will you wear? Will you include some favorite toys, musical instruments, or family pets like the Graham children did?

Swirl, Girl!

Someone's having fun!
Look closely at this dancing
scene to see if you can find:

3 top hats

1 bunch of purple plums

1 ring

1 tilted chair

1 red flower

3 mustaches

1 bunch of violets

3 straw hats

Dance at Bougival,
Pierre-Auguste Renoir (French, 1841–1919)
Museum of Fine Arts, Boston, Massachusetts, U.S.A.
Bridgeman Images

Pierre-Auguste Renoir, *Dance at Bougival*

Swirling skirts, twirling people. It's time to dance outdoors!

What time of year do you think of when you look at this painting, art sleuth? What makes you think so?

A Day in the Park

These people are enjoying a beautiful afternoon in a park just outside of Paris, France. Some artists' paintings tell us a lot about what people's lives were like in their day. Auguste Renoir was one of them. He loved to paint people, and he loved to catch them in an everyday moment. Perhaps these people just got off from work and are meeting their friends for a little music and dancing before they go home. If you visited Paris on a beautiful afternoon today, you would still find people sitting outdoors in the parks enjoying music with their friends.

Choose Your Colors

The dancing girl is wearing a pretty summer dress and a red hat. Red is the brightest color in the painting. Renoir used it because he wanted you to look at the girl first. Did you? That's something to think about when you're painting a picture. You can decide what's most important and make it stand out by choosing your colors.

Tricks of the Trade

A painting doesn't move, but when you look at this picture your eyes tell you that this couple is moving. How did Renoir do that? He had a couple of tricks that he used. Look at the hem of the girl's skirt: it's swirling the way it would if you turned around fast. The edge of the girl's hat is also blowing backward as though the air is lifting it. There's another clue to the artist's tricks, too. When you're moving fast, the things that you're passing look blurry. Renoir did that here, making the people in the background a little bit blurred. What do you think, art sleuth: Did the girl drop her bouquet because she's dancing so fast?

People Watching

You can tell that Renoir liked to look at people. He painted in details that tell you a little bit about the people in his pictures. The man sitting at the table in this painting looks like he's laughing and telling a good story. The woman with him is a good listener. The girl who's dancing looks a little shy with her eyes on the ground. The man who's dancing likes her. Do you think he's going to kiss her?

How Sweet

Fruit and cookies, yum!
But don't let them distract
you. Look closely to find:

1 green wing

1 butterfly

3 lion's heads

1 checkered handle

3 spoons

1 open lid

1 man with a spear

1 pesky fly

Still Life,
Georg Flegel (German, born in Moravia, 1563-1638)
Alte Pinakothek, Munich, Germany
Bridgeman Images

Georg Flegel, *Still Life*

Tabletops

This type of painting, called a still life, is often set up on a tabletop. In the 1500s, when Georg Flegel painted this still life, people liked to display their pretty glassware and silver, fancy flowers, and special food that they might serve only to guests. If you were painting a still life of your favorite things, what things would you include? Try arranging them on a table-top to see what they look like —and take a picture!

Look at all that food! What would you like to try first?

When you look close at a table covered with treats, there are details hidden everywhere!

Still Life/Real Life

Usually there's no sign of people in a still life, but sometimes there are other sorts of creatures—three in this picture. Did you find the fly and butterfly? Who let them in? The parrot seems to be looking right at us. A parrot was an exotic pet in Germany in the 1500s. If you made a still-life drawing of your things, would you put flies or bugs in it? How about an exotic spider? Would you want your pet to pose?

Show-Off!

A still life allows an artist to show off a little. It's tricky to paint glass that looks real, and also silver and lace and feathers and even a slice of bread! Flegel was showing people that he was clever enough to paint all of those things—in one painting. Look closely at the details of the metalwork and glass. Flegel painted all sorts of little details of flowers and faces and curlicues that look like you could feel them if you touched the painting.

What to Eat

There are so many different foods on this table. Can you name any of them? Those white candied sugar sticks in the middle look awfully sweet. Which foods look crunchy? Which look chewy? What would you like to eat? What would you want to leave on your plate?

Telltale Signs

Even though there are no people in the painting, it looks like they must be nearby. Someone lifted grapes from the plate and left them on the table. Someone took a piece of pomegranate, and someone cracked open a ______. I'll bet the parrot knows who!

Game Time

Test your memory. Study this painting for a couple of minutes. Now close your eyes. How many different foods can you remember from the painting? What did you forget? Play the game with someone else. See who can remember the most.

See You in the Garden

It's hard to hide in an open landscape, but you still might have to look closely to find:

1 basket

1 fish

1 gate

1 paintbrush

1 beard

4 black hats

1 book

1 roof (in three different places)

The Brockman Family at Beachborough,
Edward Haytley (British, active 1740–1764)
National Gallery of Victoria, Melbourne, Australia
Bridgeman Images

Edward Haytley,
The Brockman Family at Beachborough

This family's garden is as big as a park.

Hmm. That's interesting the Brockman family cows come in several different colors!

Family Portrait

The Brockman family wanted to pose in their garden, not inside their home. They are dressed up in their finest clothes. This painting tells you a little bit about the personalities of each of the people by their activities—fishing, drawing, and reading. If you wanted to tell people something about yourself in a painting, what would you be doing? Would you be dressed up in your best clothes, catching a fish?

Look!

What do you suppose the little girl is trying to say? Is she telling the lady in the blue dress that the lady in white has already caught a fish? Or is she pointing out the swans? The lady in pink has turned to look directly at the artist, just like people do in photographs. The artist is showing us part of her drawing. What has she drawn?

Off in the Distance

Edward Haytley liked to paint landscapes. When he painted this one he showed us what the park looked like as far as the eye can see. Look at how tiny and fuzzy things are in the back of the painting. It's as if you were really looking at something very far away.

Beachborough Park

This beautiful park, Beachborough, was part of the Brockman family's home in England. This painting was made over 250 years ago, but you can still visit the park today. What would you want to explore first? Would you climb inside the tiny temple at the edge of the pond or run out through that little gate into the fields to visit the sheep and cows?

Reflections

Look closely at the pond that Edward Haytley has created. It is so still that you can see many reflections. Something funny happens when things reflect in the water. They turn upside down! Look at the tree's reflection. It almost looks as though it's growing down to the bottom of the pond. What other reflections can you spot? Are they upside down, too?

Draw a portrait of your family outside. Will you be in the backyard or a beautiful park? Will you be wearing your fanciest clothes?

Let's Dance

With so many people in one place, surely there are things for an art sleuth to find. Look for:

1 drum

1 black mustache

1 row of blue buttons

1 green apron

1 group of children

2 little clouds

1 striped shawl

4 red shoes

A Centennial of Independence,
Henri Rousseau (French, 1844–1910)
Getty Museum,
Los Angeles, California, U.S.A.
Bridgeman Images

Henri Rousseau,
A Centennial of Independence

Festive decorations, a band playing, people dancing—it's a holiday!

Put on your thinking cap, art sleuth. Are the people in the circle moving to the right, or moving to the left?

Celebrate!

It's a beautiful day for a celebration in the countryside. The sky is blue with just two tiny clouds. No rain in sight! We know there's a breeze because the striped banners are blowing slightly. And with people dancing on the grass under the leafy branches of a tree, the air must smell fresh and green.

Never Give Up

Henri Rousseau lived in France more than a hundred years ago. He loved to paint as a boy, but he didn't start painting seriously until he was a grown man. He never went to art school; instead, he taught himself how to paint. Rousseau used his imagination and painted what he saw in his mind. At first people made fun of his paintings. But that didn't stop him from painting. He kept going, he never tried to paint like anyone else, and he even gave lessons to teach others to paint. Eventually, people learned to love his paintings because they were so colorful and original.

An Artist's Imagination

Rousseau had a very good imagination. Sometimes he painted scenes of wild animals in jungles that he had never seen. In this picture, he painted a scene of people celebrating an event that took place a hundred years before him! The people in the painting are not people he actually knew. They are dressed in old-fashioned costumes, not the kind of clothes that Rousseau and his friends wore. The bright colors he chose make it look like everyone is having a good time. Bright colors in a painting make a happy scene.

Let's Farandole

Did your sleuthing eyes spot the musicians in the background of this painting? The other people have joined hands to dance around the tree. The dance they are doing is called the farandole, which is done in a circle. Rousseau painted the dancers' feet hopping and kicking. Their skirts and jackets are moving with the rhythm of the music. Do you think they are moving fast or slow?

What's for Breakfast?

Bread, marmalade, cookies, and grapes: What do you think the baby will choose next for his breakfast, art sleuth? See whether you can find:

1 ball

2 spoons

2 books

3 hats

4 eggs

1 doll

1 basket

1 pair of gloves

The Breakfast,
Claude Monet (French, 1840–1926)
Städel Museum, Frankfurt-am-Main, Germany
Bridgeman Images

Claude Monet, *The Breakfast*

The nanny's waiting to take the baby in his stroller, the maid is waiting to clear the table, but first, they have to finish their breakfast!

Where's Papa?

Claude Monet painted this scene of his wife, Camille, and little son, Jean, in 1868 when he was 28 years old. Jean is the same little boy that you see in the painting on page 91. Even though you can't see Monet in this painting, he managed to include himself in it. That's his chair pulled away from the table in the foreground and his newspaper next to his plate. Do you think his eggs will get cold before he's finished painting?

How Big?

In Monet's day, great big paintings were only made for very important subjects and very important people. Family scenes were usually painted on small canvases. But Monet did the opposite here. This painting is almost 5′ (1.5 m) wide and 7.5′ (2.2 m) tall. Not only that, the star of the painting is his child. Now that's an important person!

Shhh! We're Eating.

When you look at this painting, does it make you feel as though the breakfast room is noisy or quiet? Monet used lots of browns and soft light coming through the curtain to create a quiet mood. If you wanted to draw a noisy breakfast room, what would you include? Bright colors? Lots of sunshine? Everyone laughing?

Toast and Jam?

Monet's specialty was painting scenes of ordinary people enjoying moments in everyday life. His canvases tell us a lot about what people wore, what they liked to do, and even what they liked to eat, more than a hundred years ago. If you wanted to show people a hundred years from now what breakfast was like at your house, what would you put on the table?

You Are an Art Sleuth!

You found a lot of things in this book's pictures. What else have you discovered about art? Lots!

1. Using blue and gray colors in a picture make it feel like a rainy day. (It's Raining, page 13.)
2. You can paint a picture by making lots of different colored dots close together. (Let's Go to the Park, page 16.)
3. You can make people look important by having them fill the whole painting. (Keeping Count, page 20.)
4. You can make artwork special by including portraits of your friends, family, and even yourself. (What a Crowd! page 22.)
5. You can give clues about the time of day and the time of year in a painting. (Quiet Time, page 29.)
6. You can use your imagination to draw a place you've never seen. (What's Everyone Doing? page 33.)
7. Light colors can make a picture look like there is sunshine. Dark colors can make you feel cool shade. (Lunchtime Is Over, page 36.)
8. You can make sure everyone notices the details in your paintings by surrounding dark areas with light ones. (Picnic Time, page 39.)
9. To create the feeling of distance, make things large in the foreground and then gradually smaller until they disappear. (Strap on Your Skates, page 45.)
10. To make things seem a little dangerous, use a gloomy background. (Stop, Thief! page 49.)
11. If you want to make a picture where you are on top of a hill, make yourself big, and everything below you small. (Pesky Monsters, page 53.)
12. Want to make a picture look really busy? Draw it so nothing quite fits on the page. (Beep! Honk! Beep! page 56.)
13. You can fit a lot of people in a painting by viewing them from above. (It's a Party! page 61.)
14. You can make things look hard or soft in a picture by making them shiny (hard) or fuzzy (soft). (Where Are You? page 64.)
15. You can show the wind in a picture by making flags and leaves and things blow in the breeze. (Ahoy There! page 68.)
16. You can tell something about someone's personality in a picture by including his or her pets, toys, or other favorite things. (Hold That Pose, page 73.)
17. You can make it look like people are moving in a picture by lifting the edges of their clothing, and blurring the background. (Swirl, Girl! page 77.)
18. You can tell people about your favorite things by arranging them in a still life. (How Sweet, page 80.)
19. If you show reflections in a pond, make everything upside down. (See You in the Garden, page 85.)
20. Be proud of your artwork! Stick to your own style and never give up. (Let's Dance, page 88.)
21. Soft, muted colors can create a quiet mood, while bold, bright colors can do the opposite. (The Breakfast, page 91.)

Who? What? Where? When?

1. Pierre-Auguste Renoir, *Les Parapluies* (*The Umbrellas*), circa 1881–1886, oil on canvas, 71 × 45¼" (180.3 × 114.9 cm).

   Pierre-Auguste Renoir, 1841–1919, worked first as a painter of porcelain before moving to Paris around 1861 and painting landscapes, still lifes, and portraits.

2. Georges Seurat, *A Sunday Afternoon on the Island of La Grande Jatte*, 1884–1886, oil on canvas, 81¾ × 121¼" (207.5 × 308.1 cm).

   Born in Paris, Seurat, 1859–1891, was the originator of Pointillism. The technique consisted of arranging harmonies of complementary-colored dots.

3. Quentin Metsys, *The Moneylender and His Wife*, 1514, oil on wood, 27¾ × 26⅜" (70.5 × 67 cm).

   Metsys, 1466–1530, worked in Antwerp, Belgium, a major economic capital and trading center of Europe in the 1400s.

4. Édouard Manet, *Music in the Tuileries Gardens*, 1862, oil on canvas, 30" x 46" (76 x 118 cm).

   Manet, 1832–1883, trained on a sailing vessel to Rio de Janeiro as a teenager, but he didn't take to naval life. After completing his art studies, he traveled throughout Europe to look at paintings and then opened his own studio in 1856 at the age of 24.

5. Fritz von Uhde, *The Nursery*, 1889, oil on canvas, 43½ × 54½" (110.7 × 138.5 cm).

   Born in Saxony, von Uhde, 1848–1911, was one of Germany's leading Impressionists.

6. The Florentine Master, *Thebaide* (detail), first quarter fifteenth century, tempera on wood, 31½ × 85" (80 × 216 cm).

   The Florentine Master is sometimes attributed to Fra Angelico, 1395–1455, and sometimes to Gherardo Starnina, who was born around 1360.

7. Claude Monet, *The Luncheon*, ca. 1873, oil on canvas, 63 × 79" (160 × 201 cm).

   One of the founders of the Impressionist movement, Monet, 1840–1926, was born in Paris and raised in Le Havre, where his father wanted him to become a grocer.

8. William Holman Hunt, *The Children's Holiday* (Portrait of Mrs. Thomas Fairbairn and Her Children), 1864–1865, oil on canvas, 84" x 58" (213 x 147 cm).

   Hunt earned his reputation by painting religious subjects, but this portrait idealizes Victorian family life. Thomas Fairbairn was Hunt's patron.

9. Hendrick Avercamp, *Winter Landscape with Ice Skaters* (detail), 1608, oil on wood, 30½ × 52" (77.3 × 131.9 cm).

   Born in Amsterdam, Avercamp, 1585–1634, is believed to have been deaf and mute. He spent his life painting landscapes, with a specialty in winter scenes.

10. Georges de La Tour, *The Fortune Teller*, ca. 1630, oil on canvas, 40⅛ × 48⅝" (102 × 123 cm).

    De La Tour, 1593–1652, worked in Lunéville, in northern France. He is known for bringing dramatic lighting to his scenes, often with the use of candlelight.

11. Hieronymus Bosch, *The Temptation of Saint Anthony*, 1490, oil on wood, 29 × 20⅝" (73 × 52.5 cm).

    Although he lived all his life in or near Brabant, the Netherlands, Bosch, 1450–1516, was known throughout Europe during his lifetime.

12. Charles Ginner, *Piccadilly Circus*, 1912, oil on canvas, 26 × 31⅝" (66 × 81.3 cm).

    Ginner, 1878–1952, is celebrated for his scenes of London, but he was born and raised in the south of France.

13. Pieter Brueghel the Younger, *The Peasants' Wedding*, date unknown, 14¼ × 17⅜" (36.2 × 44.2 cm).

    Brueghel the Younger, circa 1564–1636, came from a very talented family of Flemish artists. He is best known for his depictions of village life.

14. Jacques (James) Tissot, *Hide and Seek*, 1877, oil on wood, 21¼ × 28⅞" (53.9 × 73.4 cm).

    Tissot, 1836–1902, was a successful painter in Paris before he moved to London, where he painted society portraits.

15. Vittore Carpaccio, *The Arrival of Saint Ursula*, 1498, oil on canvas, 110 × 100" (280 × 255 cm).

    Carpaccio, 1465–1525/26, was the painter of scenes of his native Venice. The Arrival of Saint Ursula is one in a series of nine large paintings he completed to tell Ursula's story.

16. William Hogarth, *The Graham Children*, 1742, oil on canvas, 63 × 71¼" (160 × 181 cm).

    Hogarth, 1697–1764, was well known for his portraiture. *The Graham Children* is one of his masterpieces.

17. Pierre-Auguste Renoir, *Dance at Bougival*, 1883, oil on canvas, 71⅝ × 38⅝" (181.9 × 98.1 cm).

    Bougival, a suburb of Paris on the Seine, was the site of open-air cafés, where the public could dance and enjoy music. Renoir, 1841–1919, did some of his best figure painting there.

18. Georg Flegel, *Still Life*, 1630, oil on wood, 8⅝ × 11" (22 × 28 cm).

    Flegel, 1563–1638, worked from Frankfurt. Nearly all his works are still lifes featuring tables covered with good things to eat.

19. Edward Haytley, *The Brockman Family at Beachborough*, 1744, oil on canvas, 20¾ × 25⅝" (52.7 × 65 cm).

    Very little is known about Haytley. He was British, is thought to have lived in the area of Lancashire, and painted between 1740 and 1764.

20. Henri Rousseau, *A Centennial of Independence*, 1892, oil on canvas, 44 × 62¼" (111.8 × 158.1 cm).

    The French naïve artist Rousseau, 1844–1910, captured a folk dance from the south of France in this painting that commemorates the 100th anniversary of the first French Republic.

21. Claude Monet, *The Breakfast*, 1868, oil on canvas, 60" x 91" (152 x 231 cm).

    The Salon de Paris rejected this painting for exhibition, along with many other Impressionists' paintings. It led the artists to create their own exhibition society, The Anonymous Society of Painters, Sculptors, and Engravers.

Answer Key

Did you find everything you were looking for, art sleuth? If you want to double-check, here's the place to do it.

It's Raining pages 10–13

Les Parapluies, Auguste Renoir

- 11 hands
- 8 hats
- 2 gloves
- 1 pocket handkerchief
- 9 umbrellas
- 2 white shirt cuffs
- 1 bracelet
- 3 beards

Let's Go to the Park

pages 14–17

A Sunday Afternoon on the Island of La Grande Jatte, Georges Seurat

- 3 dogs
- 1 trumpet
- 2 fishing poles
- 1 folding fan
- 1 monkey
- 1 bouquet
- 9 open parasols
- 1 butterfly

Keeping Count

pages 18–21

The Moneylender and His Wife, Quentin Metsys

3 windows
4 hats
6 rings
1 candle
2 rolls of paper
1 red button
1 glass bottle
1 brick wall

What a Crowd! pages 22–25

Music in the Tuileries Gardens, Édouard Manet

1 dog
2 fans
4 parasols
1 spoon
1 cane
2 pairs of eyeglasses
5 black shoes
1 ball

Quiet Time pages 26–29

The Nursery, Fritz von Uhde

1 dog
1 clock
1 stool
1 bonnet
1 doll hat
1 tiny house
7 dolls
★ the number 2

What's Everyone Doing?

pages 30–33

***Thebaide* (detail),** The Florentine Master, attributed to Fra Angelico

1 fox
4 caves
3 faces in windows
5 books
1 fish
3 riders
2 baskets
1 tiny castle

Lunchtime Is Over

pages 34–37

The Luncheon, Claude Monet

1 hat with white roses
1 hat with red trim
2 drinking glasses
1 open parasol
1 closed parasol
2 fruit bowls
1 wooden toy
★ the loaf's missing piece of bread

Picnic Time

pages 38–41

The Children's Holiday, William Holman Hunt

1 blue bow
1 berry necklace
1 peach in hand
1 ring
1 basket
1 headband
2 spoons
★ a hat that's turned into a bowl

Strap on Your Skates

pages 42–45

Winter Landscape with Ice Skaters, Hendrick Avercamp

3 horses
1 missing hat
1 ladder
1 boat with a sail
1 oar
1 axe
1 sign with a crescent moon
1 horse with a plume

Stop, Thief! pages 46–49

The Fortune Teller, Georges de La Tour

1 coin
2 rabbits
1 earring
1 clipper
1 gold bracelet
2 birds
1 knife in a sheath
1 gold clasp

Pesky Monsters
pages 50–53

The Temptation of Saint Anthony, Hieronymus Bosch

2 ladders
1 tiny bow and arrow
1 spilling jug
1 armed funnel
3 bridges
2 bells
★ Anthony's eyeglasses
★ the letter T

Beep! Honk! Beep!
pages 54–57

Piccadilly Circus, Charles Ginner

5 wheels
1 green hat
1 steering wheel
1 white hat band
3 lamps
1 white collar
★ the number 19 twice
★ the word "room"

It's a Party! pages 58–61

The Peasants' Wedding,
Pieter Brueghel the Younger

1 pen and paper
1 bird
8 red hats
1 pair of knee socks
1 set of folded arms in front
1 set of folded arms in back
1 baby
2 purses on strings

Where Are You?
pages 62–65

Hide and Seek,
Jacques (James) Tissot

4 children
1 open door
2 headbands
3 mirrors
2 teacups
1 black shoe
3 masks
★ a wrinkle in the rug

Ahoy There! pages 66–69

The Arrival of Saint Ursula,
Vittore Carpaccio

1 red dog collar
1 bird
1 man on a mast
1 round roof
2 pieces of paper
2 feathered helmets
1 man on a bridge
★ some people in windows

Hold That Pose

pages 70–73

The Graham Children, William Hogarth

2 gray ears
1 tiny angel
2 birds
1 wheel
1 cookie
2 buckles
2 bunches of cherries
1 pointed toe

Swirl, Girl! pages 74–77

Dance at Bougival,
Pierre-Auguste Renoir

3 top hats
1 bunch of purple plums
1 ring
1 tilted chair
1 red flower
3 mustaches
1 bunch of violets
3 straw hats

How Sweet pages 78–81

Still Life, Georg Flegel

1 green wing
1 butterfly
3 lion's heads
1 checkered handle
3 spoons
1 open lid
1 man with a spear
1 pesky fly

See You in the Garden

pages 82–85

The Brockman Family at Beachborough, Edward Haytley

1 basket
1 fish
1 gate
1 paintbrush
1 beard
4 black hats
1 book
1 roof (in three different places)

Let's Dance

pages 86–89

A Centennial of Independence, Henri Rousseau

1 drum
1 black mustache
1 row of blue buttons
1 green apron
1 group of children
2 little clouds
1 striped shawl
4 red shoes

What's for Breakfast?

pages 90–93

The Breakfast, Claude Monet

1 ball
2 spoons
2 books
3 hats
4 eggs
1 doll
1 basket
1 pair of gloves

About the Author

Brooke DiGiovanni Evans is a museum educator currently serving as head of gallery learning at the Museum of Fine Arts, Boston. For fifteen years, she has been teaching children and adults in art, history, and science museums. She holds an Ed.M. from Harvard University.